# Cornell Notebook
with
# Sketchnoting

## Cornell

Format

with

Visual Note-taking

## (Sketchnoting)

methodology

added.

# Cornell Notebook with Sketchnoting

This Notebook combines Cornell note-taking pages and the Cornell note taking methods with visual note-taking methods in order to enhance and improve a students note taking and study techniques.

## CORNELL METHOD

The Cornell method provides a systematic format for condensing and organizing notes. A study published in the summer of 2013 found that; "Students who were taught to use the Cornell method did take better notes than those who did not." This is however not a guarantee of better academic achievement.

## VISUAL METHOD

**Visual notetaking** or sketchnoting is a process of representing ideas non-linguistically. (By "drawing pictures.") ... Whether simple or complex, **visual** notes can be used to more deeply process information as well as communicate it to others with images.
If you're a visual learner with a passion for pens and paper, a visual note-taking method is perfect for you. Visual note-taking combines traditional handwritten notes with drawings, symbols, and other creative elements. The result is an engaging map of ideas with clear visual cues.
Using visual methods, you can:
- Boost memory retention
- Keep your brain active, engaged and stimulated
- Make your notes more compact and easier to review

    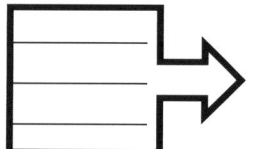

# Effectiveness in Class

## 1. Go to class prepared

"Always have a plan and believe in it. Nothing good happens by accident." — Chuck Knox, NFL football coach

- Choose Your Seat Carefully - Most people attending classes don't really care where they sit. They may be influenced by where their friends are sitting, or they may position themselves at the back in case they decide to bail on the talk halfway through. Choose a strategic vantage point where you can obtain the best notes. This usually means sitting in the front row, so you have no visual obstacles and no sound distortions between you and the information source.

- Prepare to take notes the same way each time. An essential question at the top of the page focuses the learner on the key learning objective that they should be able to discuss upon leaving the class

- When using a bound notebook, have a plan for how you will handle handouts, other class resources or your own out-of-class notes and insure that they are added to your notes in the correct order. You may want to have tape handy so that you can insert these documents.

- Bring highlighters and colored pens or markers to class. When instructors say "This is important." Or, "Make sure you understand this." It will more than likely be on an exam. Highlighting these notes will help remind you later that this is something you need to know.

- Read assigned material and previous class notes before class. Make your own notations about material or concepts that you think are important or that you don't quite understand. You will then have a better understanding of what the instructor says. This will give you a better chance to identify important points.

## 2. Improve your listening skills.

"The art of effective listening is essential to clear communication." James Cash Penney

- Enter the classroom with a positive attitude. This allows you to be open-minded and enables you to get the most out of the information presented.

- Make a conscious effort to pay attention. Concentrate on listening.

- Learn how to listen for important information versus trivial information.

- Take cues from the lecturer or source, e.g. "This is important…"

- Latch Onto Quotes - Whether they are key phrases you hear the presenter say, or quotes by other people that the presenter references. They are often poignant summaries of a topic, and you should listen carefully for them. When you hear one that resonates or beautifully summarises the point being made, jot it down and wrap it in some fancy talking marks or a speech balloon.

- Develop skills to use when the lecture becomes empty space. Develop a plan for how you will use your time in situations where someone asks a question which you have no interest in or on a subject that you are very comfortable with. Your attention could drift off, but you don't want to miss important information before you realize that the lecturer is back on track. Have a plan for what you will be doing in these situations. Go back and modify or clarify your diagrams?

# Effectiveness in Class

## 3. Develop a notetaking method that works for you.

Plan the structure and organization of your notes.

- Start each new lecture on a new page, and date and number each page. The sequence of material is important.

- Write on one side of the paper only. This will come in handy when reviewing or studying for exams.

- Space out your notes. Don't write on every line. This allows you to add comments or note questions later.

- Make your notes as brief as possible. Never use a sentence when you can use a phrase, or a phrase when you can use a word or a word when you can use a picture. Use bullet points and lists where possible.

- Take notes in your own words – paraphrase what you hear so it makes sense to you rather than write down verbatim what is said.

- Develop your own system of abbreviations and symbols that you can use wherever possible.

- Use highlighters and color to indicate key ideas, changes in concepts or links between information.

- Note all unfamiliar vocabulary or concepts you don't understand. This reminds you to look them up later.

- Take Advantage Of Down Time. Most lectures will have intense moments followed by slower sections. This light and shade is the mark of a good presentation, but it's also an opportunity for you. If you hear something *important but lengthy* during an intense moment, and don't want to lose your concentration, jot down the one phrase that summarises the moment. Then, during lulls in the presentation, you can embellish your notes

## 4. Pay close attention to content.

Knowing what and how much to write down is sometimes difficult. Rely on some of the following tips for what to include in your notes.

- Details, facts, or explanations that explain main points. Add examples. Include:
    - Definitions
    - Lists or bullet points.
    - Material written on the chalkboard or on a transparency, including drawings or charts.
    - Information that is repeated or spelled out.
- Connect key chunks of material in your notes using color or symbols

# Effectiveness in Class

## 5. Review and edit your notes.

Authorities on effective study skills consider reviewing and editing class notes to be the most important part of notetaking and essential to increasing learning capacity.

- Review your notes within 24 hours.

- Edit with a different colored pen to distinguish between what you wrote in class and what you filled in later.

- Use the "Key Points" column of your Cornell sheet to expand on or highlight important information.

- Highlight information that you don't fully understand to remind you to do further study or ask your instructor.

- Compare your notes with the textbook reading and fill in important details in the blank spaces you left.

- Exchange ideas and collaborate with other students to check for understanding and test the comprehensiveness of each other's notes.

- Reflect over an entire unit (Thoughtful Review) on a regular basis prior to and leading up to exams and tests.

## Retaining Information

Retaining information involves active rather than passive learning. Active learning places the responsibility for learning on the learner. Studies have found that note taking is most effective when notes are organised and transformed in some way. An effective note-taking strategy requires effort. Half the battle is understanding the reasons for taking notes and interacting regularly with your notes.

# Effectiveness in Class

## Sketchnoting

The term sketchnoting describes the style of visual note-taking that has become popular at tech conferences. But regardless of the forum, the tool is valuable. Here are a few guidelines for creating sketchnotes:

## 1. Tool Up

While it's not essential to use an expensive art pen or trendy notepads, you don't want to start off ill equipped. Spend a few bucks on the minimum amount of resources:

- A notebook large enough so that you won't feel restricted by space.
- Reasonable quality black felt tip pens. You may want to experiment with different tip diameters to find one that fits your style
- Additional colored pens for highlighting.
- Correction fluid. You may just need to change the source or destination of an arrow.

## 2. Master Sketching Common Objects

It's useful to have a cache of objects in your repertoire, ready to pull out as needed. In most subjects, there are certain important words or phrases that will crop up time and again. Practice visual representations for these in advance, so you don't get flustered trying to draw them for the first time in the middle of a talk. Here are some suggestions:

- **Basic shapes:** stars, squares, rectangles, triangles, circles,
- **Basic objects:** ship, home, fish, user, cloud, link, hand, mouse, book, newspaper, magazine, tree, envelope, brick, brain, magnifying glass, pencil, paper, scissors, knife, fork, spoon,

## 3. Use Creative Containers

There are a ton of simple containers that you can use to chunk text in a way that is visually interesting and easily understood. Consider speech bubbles, thought clouds, sound effect containers, dotted-line rules, double-border rectangles.

## 4. Use Creative Connectors

While containers are useful for isolating chunks of text, connectors are used to group those chunks together. Arrows are the most common connectors, but there's no reason you couldn't include a range of swirly flourishes. Experiment and invent your own connectors.

## 5. Apply Shading & Color

- highlight text
- color in containers, for visual contrast
- the list goes on…

Some people also like to include color, to highlight text, draw attention to parts of a sketch or make key concepts lift from the page. The key to color is not overdoing it—when in doubt,

## 6. Find Your Own Style

Be proud of your sketches, refer to them regularly, and you'll see an original style evolve.

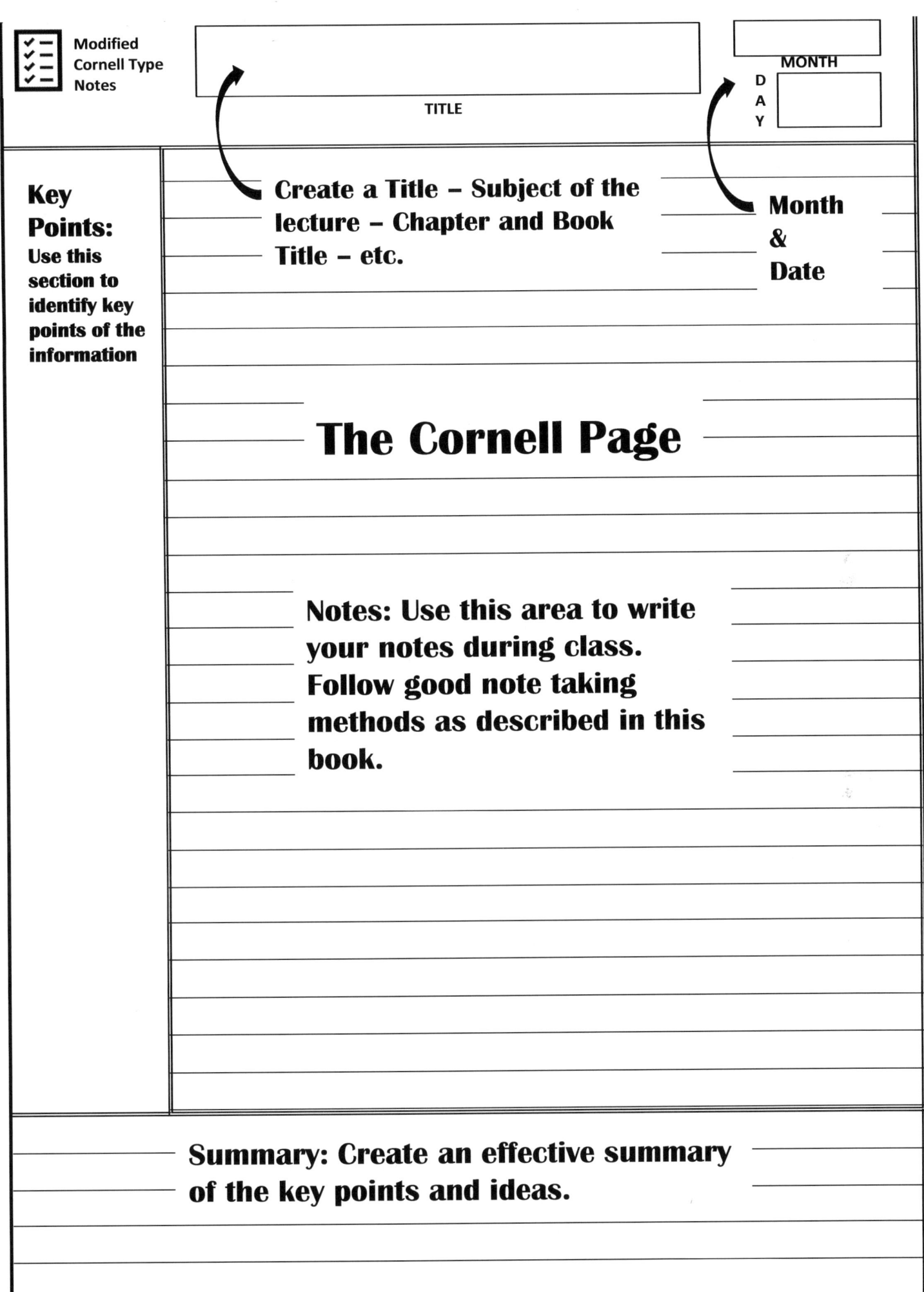

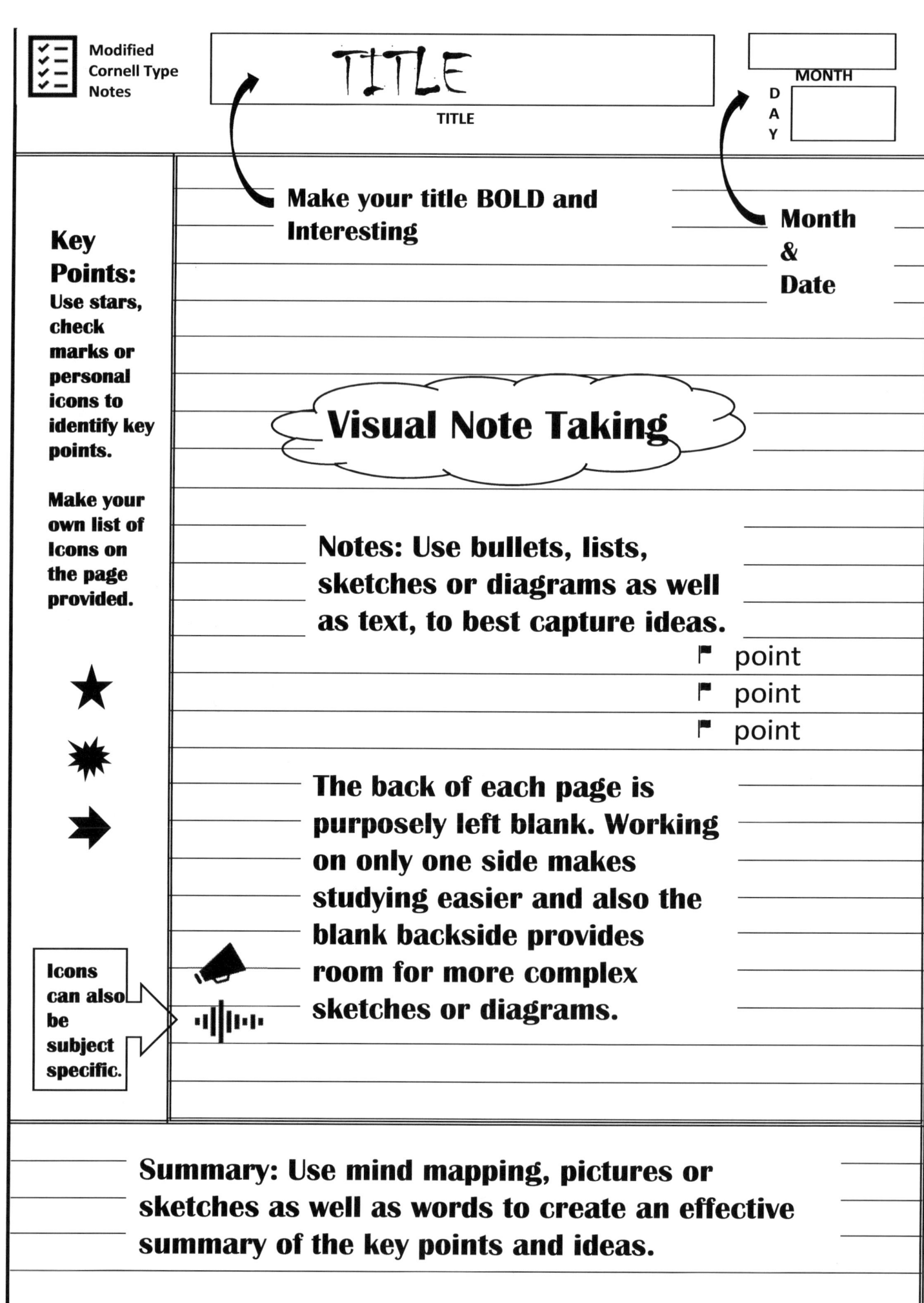

**SAMPLE**

**Title:** 111 MILLION TON PROBLEM (111,000,000)
**Month:** JUNE
**Day:** 21/18

*Modified Cornell Type Notes*

| Cues | Notes |
|---|---|
| NEW WASTE → | CHINA HAS 106,000,000 TONS OF PLASTIC FROM ALL OVER THE WORLD. 111 MILLION BY 2030. NEW WASTE BAGS, BOTTLES, WRAPPERS. $57.6 BILLION WORTH SINCE 1992. THE WORLD HAS CREATED 8.1 BILLION TONS OF PLASTIC SINCE 2017. |
| (earth sketch) | 8.1 BILLION TONS — 4/5 GOES TO LANDFILLS. |
| HELP! (dolphin, happy/sad faces) | 7,000,000 TONS GOES INTO OCEANS EVERY YEAR. 14,000,000,000 lbs |
| | 9% HAS BEEN RECYCLED — **ONLY**. |
| ☆ | **2017 CHINA WILL STOP TAKING EVERYONE ELSES PLASTIC** |
| | [ PLASTIC PRODUCED | PLASTIC RECYCLED / PLASTIC BURIED | ? ] |

**Summary:** The world has a problem! We produce lots of plastic. We only reuse a small amount. China who took a lot of it will stop.

## MY ICONS  →  Subject Specific ↓

| | KEY POINT | | ____ |
| | KEY PERSON | | ____ |
| | NEED ADDITIONAL STUDY | | ____ |
| | KEY QUESTION | | ____ |
| | EMPHASIS BY INSTRUCTOR | | ____ |
| | ____ | | ____ |

*Create your own unique icons. Make them easy and quick to use. Examples: ⭐ Key Point, ☺ Key Person, 👓 Need Additional Study*

**Modified Cornell Type Notes**

**TITLE**

**MONTH**
**DAY**

**Modified Cornell Type Notes**

**Modified Cornell Type Notes**

TITLE

MONTH
DAY

Modified Cornell Type Notes

TITLE

MONTH
DAY

**Modified Cornell Type Notes**

TITLE

MONTH
DAY

Modified Cornell Type Notes

**TITLE**

**MONTH**

**DAY**

**Modified Cornell Type Notes**

TITLE

MONTH
DAY

Modified Cornell Type Notes

**Modified Cornell Type Notes**

TITLE

MONTH
DAY

**Modified Cornell Type Notes**

**Modified Cornell Type Notes**

**TITLE**

MONTH
DAY

**Modified Cornell Type Notes**

Modified Cornell Type Notes

**TITLE**

**MONTH**
DAY

Modified Cornell Type Notes

**TITLE**

**MONTH**
DAY

Modified Cornell Type Notes

**TITLE**

**MONTH**
**DAY**

**Modified Cornell Type Notes**

**TITLE**

**MONTH**
**DAY**

**Modified Cornell Type Notes**

**TITLE**

**MONTH**
**DAY**

**Modified Cornell Type Notes**

TITLE

MONTH
DAY

**Modified Cornell Type Notes**

**Modified Cornell Type Notes**

**TITLE**

**MONTH**
**DAY**

**Modified Cornell Type Notes**

**Modified Cornell Type Notes**

**TITLE**

**MONTH**
**DAY**

**Modified Cornell Type Notes**

**Modified Cornell Type Notes**

**TITLE**

**MONTH**
**DAY**

**Modified Cornell Type Notes**

**TITLE**

**MONTH**

**DAY**

**Modified Cornell Type Notes**

TITLE

MONTH
DAY

**Modified Cornell Type Notes**

**TITLE**

**MONTH**
**DAY**

**Modified Cornell Type Notes**

**TITLE**

**MONTH**
**DAY**

**Modified Cornell Type Notes**

**TITLE**

**MONTH**
**DAY**

Modified Cornell Type Notes

TITLE

MONTH
DAY

Modified Cornell Type Notes

**TITLE**

MONTH
DAY

**Modified Cornell Type Notes**

**TITLE**

**MONTH**
**DAY**

**Modified Cornell Type Notes**

**TITLE**

**MONTH**
**DAY**

**Modified Cornell Type Notes**

TITLE

MONTH
DAY

**Modified Cornell Type Notes**

TITLE

MONTH
D
A
Y

**Modified Cornell Type Notes**

TITLE

MONTH
DAY

**Modified Cornell Type Notes**

TITLE

MONTH
DAY

**Modified Cornell Type Notes**

**TITLE**

**MONTH**
**DAY**

**Modified Cornell Type Notes**

TITLE

MONTH
DAY

**Modified Cornell Type Notes**

**TITLE**

**MONTH**
**DAY**

**Modified Cornell Type Notes**

**TITLE**

**MONTH**
**DAY**

**Modified Cornell Type Notes**

**TITLE**

**MONTH**
**DAY**

**Modified Cornell Type Notes**

TITLE

MONTH
DAY

**Modified Cornell Type Notes**

**TITLE**

**MONTH**
**DAY**

**Modified Cornell Type Notes**

**TITLE**

**MONTH**
**DAY**

**Modified Cornell Type Notes**

**TITLE**

**MONTH**
**DAY**

**Modified Cornell Type Notes**

TITLE

MONTH
DAY

**Modified Cornell Type Notes**

**TITLE**

**MONTH**
**DAY**

Modified Cornell Type Notes

TITLE

MONTH
DAY

**Modified Cornell Type Notes**

TITLE

MONTH
DAY

**Modified Cornell Type Notes**

**TITLE**

**MONTH**
**DAY**

**Modified Cornell Type Notes**

TITLE

MONTH
DAY

**Modified Cornell Type Notes**

**TITLE**

**MONTH**
**DAY**

Modified Cornell Type Notes

**TITLE**

**MONTH**
DAY

**Modified Cornell Type Notes**

TITLE

MONTH
DAY

Modified Cornell Type Notes

**TITLE**

**MONTH**
**DAY**

**Modified Cornell Type Notes**

TITLE

MONTH
DAY

**Modified Cornell Type Notes**

TITLE

MONTH
DAY

**Modified Cornell Type Notes**

TITLE

MONTH
DAY

**Modified Cornell Type Notes**

TITLE

MONTH
DAY

Modified Cornell Type Notes

**TITLE**

**MONTH**
DAY

**Modified Cornell Type Notes**

**TITLE**

**MONTH**
**DAY**

**Modified Cornell Type Notes**

**TITLE**

**MONTH**
**DAY**

Made in the USA
Lexington, KY
02 November 2018